ANNA ROBINSON was born and lives in London. She has an MA in Public History from Ruskin College, Oxford. Her pamphlet, *Songs from the Flats*, was a Poetry Book Society Pamphlet Choice. She was the first recipient of The Poetry School Scholarship and her poetry was featured in the School's second anthology, *Entering the Tapestry* (Enitharmon Press, 2003). Her work has appeared in several journals and anthologies, including *Poetry London, Brittle Star, In The Company of Poets* (Hearing Eye, 2003) and *Oxford Poets 2007*. As part of Poetry International and the South Bank Centre's Trading Places project, Robinson was Poet in Residence in Lower Marsh in 2006. A former tutor in prisons, she is a regular poetry judge for the Koestler Competition and is a founding editor for *Not Shut Up!* and the newly established *Long Poem Magazine*.

Anna Robinson

THE FINDERS OF LONDON

ENITHARMON PRESS

First published in 2010
by Enitharmon Press
26B Caversham Road
London NW5 2DU

www.enitharmon.co.uk

Distributed in the UK by
Central Books
99 Wallis Road
London E9 5LN

Distributed in the USA and Canada
by Dufour Editions Inc.
PO Box 7, Chester Springs
PA 19425, USA

ISBN: 978-1-904634-94-2

Enitharmon Press gratefully acknowledges the financial support of
Arts Council England, London.

British Library Cataloguing-in-Publication Data.
A catalogue record for this book is available
from the British Library.

Volume 4 in the Enitharmon New Poets series,
dedicated to the memory of Alan Clodd (1918–2002)
and generously funded by his estate.

Designed by Libanus Press
and printed in England by
CPI Antony Rowe

ACKNOWLEDGEMENTS

These poems have been published in: *And Then There Was Light* (The Way of Words), *Brando's Hat, Brittle Star, Entering the Tapestry* (Enitharmon Press), *In the Company of Poets* (Hearing Eye Press), *www.longpoemmagazine.org.uk*, *www.poetrypf.co.uk*, *Magma, Murray Street* (The Poetry School), *Oxford Poets Anthology 2007* (Carcanet Press), *Plant Care: A Festschrift for Mimi Khalvati* (Linda Lee Books), *Poetry London, Reactions 4* (pen&inc), *the reater 4* (Wrecking Ball Press), *Songs from the Flats* (Hearing Eye Press), *South Bank Magazine, Trading Places* (Spread the Word).

'Charlie's Dead' and 'Lower Marsh Speaks' were written in response to a commission from Spread the Word and the South Bank Centre in 2006.

I would like to thank my family and friends and staff from the following archives: Lambeth Archives, London Metropolitan Archives, National Archives. I would also like to thank my teachers, especially Mimi Khalvati.

CONTENTS

for my family, alive and in spirit, and for the beach

LENTEN MOON

Above the plane tree in the park and moving fast – Lenten Moon –
you silence the birds with fullness. Down here – it's my neighbour's
birthday; we sing and laugh not fasting much at all – and you – crisp
as a crust moon, crow and sugar moon, light the yard.

Chaste Moon, they've got you wrong, you're not spotless, your
man-scars are vivid and dark. Stories of how the crow flies, birds
that become rabbits, the child that spoke and how we nearly died
laughing, get told in the dark crisp air. Are you impressed? You're
clear of the chimneys now and rising.

'WHAT IS MORE BEAUTIFUL THAN A ROAD?'

Georges Sand

It's raining. We talk, here, where we always talk.
Where the pavement flares roundly in front of the Action Centre.
Next door is a caff; we never go there.
The rain started as you told me what the worst thing is for you.
It was gentle then but now we are really wet and you don't seem to have
noticed.
At my shoulder are my Grandmas and behind them, their Grandmas.
They stand, a long line of women getting wet on street corners.
None of us are dreaming of stairs.

CHARLIE'S DEAD

There she is – the young ghost –
slipping through the gaps
between the buildings where roads
used to be. She is fast
and her skirt flicks with her and she has
so much to keep in check.

Today, she's wearing her work skirt –
black, knee-length, straight.
It's doing battle with a once-white
nylon tube that's fighting
its way down, clinging to the backs
of her stockings while it goes.

It is static – so no use to her
in a hurry, as always.
Once I saw her in ankle-length worsted –
again work-black, again straight –
and the white lace peaked from beneath
one whole inch above

her boot-lace – and she cut out –
where the alley had been –
to hoist the too-white frill back up
from the waistband and fix with a pin
that was bent to breaking. She is always
at half-mast and struggling.

GOSCRATCHYERSELF
i.m. Aunt Beat

Wha'dus she mean? Is she chuckin' ya'rin, fa' ya' sawce –
to tha| room where no wun stayz, if they don'| 'av ta,

are ya' bein' mayd ta si| on a sowfa, oose faydin' pa|ern leaps
sudden-like acrosh'ya – wiv a ping you can almost 'ear –

fayverin' yur'ankles an' wrists – or is she callin' you a mu| –
or a pigeon, or any beast ov'a fiyald – or is she suggestin' maybe

you dohn'| wash? She is 'avin' a larff. 'Er fin showlders movin'
inside 'er lemon cardigan, which is nylon an' noo an' very clean.

Meanwhile a ghost of 'erself is bizy in the upstairs room, pu|ing
moff-balls in 'er slippers, wrappin' 'er good skir| in wax paypa.

THE PANSY POEMS

Pansy Neilson's Magnificent

This is not the leper house,
it's not here that lesions creep
through a bright red haze.

That's on the other side –
where they've put builders' huts
over the football pitch.

What is this haze – smudging out
from the blotch to form a margin?
It's red as in heart not iron –

or blood – a red too Victorian
to stand for this place,
too red for the likes of us.

Renovations

It's foolish to think there'd be no conflict;
the scaffold closes in on us, blocks

the light-stream and it doesn't rain.
Our pansies are dead. They will not regenerate.

The cold new doors come: too fast, too heavy
and we're stuck behind them, eye to little eye,

stomach driven, planning our resistance;
but the new windows will not break

and we've forgotten how to destroy steel.
The landladies talk of how nice it will be,

how much we'll like it when it's done.
On Fridays we blow their dust off our tools.

I rub my saw, my iron mallet,
my neighbour shines up his hammer.

The empty baskets and window boxes avoid
our eyes. Yes, we're waiting, we are waiting.

Show Pansies

The blooms should be thick and circular,
no waviness in the petals, they should
possess a glossy, velvet appearance.
In Kill 'em and Eat 'em Street, we watch.

The face of the bloom should be slightly
arched or convex, with a small eye.
The dustbin lids have gone missing again.

The two centre petals should meet above
and reach well up on the top two.
The landladies are on the roof.

The lower petal should be sufficiently
deep and broad for balance and each
should lie evenly upon the others.
They can't find them either.

To elaborate further, the top of the lower
petal should be straight and flat.
But look what they've spotted.

The two centre petals should be arranged
evenly on either side of an imaginary
line drawn through the yellow eye.
Someone's hanging out washing at Number 3.

The top of these petals should reach to the same
height on the upper petals so that the whole
of the bloom is evenly balanced.
It isn't Monday. Someone will pay.

On the Landing

Red, cream, a sink with a cold tap
the eye on each landing
collecting water
us under the table
the eye – the sink with a cold tap
always yellow
the worries, the petals
those were the days
Aunty through the window
the flats become colour
we meet where we collect water
by the eye
on the landing
the block – hit by fire
always yellow
but the petals, always cream
always red
Victorian to the touch
tough as tongues
there's a margin in the brickwork
a sink with a cold tap
and the eye, always yellow

Ghosting

I wake where I was sleeping
in my room
but the walls are gone
and all I see are night shapes
twisting away from the bed.
They're brambles, I think,
yes, they are, and in full fruit
and now I can feel the night's a warm one
and now I can feel there is no breeze.

Trying to find my bearings
by the moon
and the brown-mirrored rear
of the Department of Health
always to its right
which has gone, like the fence
to the park, like the park and the flats
and now I can see the shape of out-house
and now I can see the moon on glass.

I get up and not finding
my slippers
walk on through grass,
which in part is boggy,
which is not such a bad thing,
and, as it's a full moon,
I see the flowers, waiting to sleep,
Viola tricolor, tickle me fancy,
heartsease, jump up and kiss me.

THE FLATS

The cats know their lands, which bit of yard
is theirs, and the lie of corridors, across
shed roofs where they can freely pass

down by the back of the Rec. and I know mine.
My corners are the nettle patch and by
the bins, our common ground the washing line.

My neighbour said *in those days we never
had kitchens, we'd cook everything on the range.*
The ghost of my hearth has moved next door,

I can hear her playing that trumpet into the night.
My neighbour said *in those days you couldn't
afford holidays.* My neighbour sleep-walks, but not

in the back yard, that's mostly my patch. She walks
round her bedroom, down the hallway, feeling,
looking for that fifth room, the one without a door.

My neighbour said *the caretakers used to decorate
your indoors. They had a book with three sorts
of wallpaper.* If we neighbours see each other

in the street we say *Oo-oo!* and flick a hand
as if we were dancing – or waiting to –
sometimes we only mouth it – but still we dance.

My neighbour said *Monday mornings down here,
women used to come out with prams loaded
with stuff: suits, watch-chains, whatever,*

*and go down the pawn shop – it was the norm.
Years ago* said my neighbour *you never
had mains electricity.* My neighbour's door

is black, like mine. My neighbour gave me a recipe:
'Where the bread though stale is in good shape,
butter and make sandwiches with left-over meat.

Beat an egg, dip and fry in good lard, send
to the table with lettuce and watercress'.
My neighbour, who shall remain nameless, said

Don't tell no one but there was once a man
whose sister lived down here, and he was killed;
and how they done it was they'd held him down

and made him swallow the bracelet that he'd bought
his lady-friend. Choked him. He didn't know,
but she was married and her husband was not

the sort you cross. In those days you could leave
your door unlocked. We've got wildlife in our yard,
self-seeding, wind-loving but we also have pansies.

He let himself in said my neighbour
and there on the table was a dinner plate
on it was kippers and he said, Oh no

not bleedin' kippers again – and then
the neighbour came through and said, 'Sod off
to your own bleedin' flat!' See, in them

days all the keys was the same – *all the doors* –
there was only one lock, it wasn't his dinner.
My neighbour was telling me all about the war.

It has rained for three days; the yard is empty
except for us, some snails and the pansies.
My neighbour says *I could murder a cup of tea.*

Tonight I wobble, trying to find you. Egg moon, fish moon –
where are you? Not in the usual place above the park – nor even
out the front to the left of the Department of Health. My blood
is too rich. I cross the road to where the pale men tremble and
even in their patch, I cannot see you.

Ah, there you are! Hiding behind the Mission, large and low
and so red tonight that all anyone can do is stare. Hooded boys
pass quickly. Seed moon, fish moon – my legs are bare, there is
benzoin on my fingers, your hare stirs in its sleep.

AS A FOOT PASSENGER ON THE WOOLWICH FERRY
after Rabelais

Sitting below deck in the cast iron holds –
sun beaming in from the west – horns calling out –
we hear – whispering voices – echoes – fog –
    all overlapping each other.

Where do they come from – are they ferry ghosts –
voices of those transported to the other world –
is this a kind of Thames triangle where people go
    and come to their own tempo?

No, says the master, these whispers are the frozen
voices of winter's passengers – slowly defrosting
on summer's breeze – listen – mah, mah, sh, op,
    bh, kuh, ush, sh, oomm.

We try to catch hold of them – skidding as we go
trap some by the stairwell – in the broad of the bow
one man catches 'mah' – wraps it in foil –
    later, he lets it go.

OPERATION AT ST THOMAS' HOSPITAL FOR POOR WOMEN

I am moving yet tied down. I am blindfold
yet know they're here, feel their eyes
shame my body, not with lust but watchfulness.
These might be my last words and no one is listening.

I am cold in my fever. They wipe my forehead.
The sky is near yet I know this is a room,
can smell the dust. I think the roof is glass,
like the chapel in the workhouse.

They wipe my forehead. They cut.
Chest tears, bones scream *Oh* and *God*.
No pain is like this, not disease, not children.
They wipe my forehead. I am so tired.

There are stars, tiny and silver, and a pale
blue light washes me. I am leaving, I feel it.
Leaving through this gap in my chest
as if I am just what I breathe.

CROSS BONES – SOUTHWARK

You crave the bones of me, I know,
would stroke them if you could but reach.
You breathe them in your dusty sleep
and fill your head with facts, I know.

You see yourself in me, I know,
like we were one across the breach.
I stir your crow to punter me
you do not feel his peck – I know.

But when we meet in flesh and blood,
my hooded child in front of me,
fog rises from the river sludge,
becomes so thick you cannot see
and so you do not recognise
the hand that holds the kitchen knife.

Annie, tha li|e is bri|e na, tee time, Sun dee.
The au|umn sky, sa'clear i|ad brayk yur'art.
What'a'ya lookin' a| ow|ov'our windda?
Dus'yur'eye skip tha workshops: boo|s,
charndler's, tin pla|e, all cloze| today, all pars|
their bes|, always there? Maybe you ain't
even lookin' a| tha bird-seller – also cloze|,
although his birds don'| soun' bovvered –
maybe you're lookin' ta see if tha frie' fish shop
is open ye|. Or are ya si|es se| 'igher?
'Air much sky can ya'see abuv the roof tops?
'Air far? Can ya'see the trams on Wa|erloo Rowd?

I carn'|. Thay've gorn' na. Anywaye, thay've bil|
a bildin', offices, for the 'elf, where them shops
yous'ta be, saym size as the ol' prin| works
but tawller and instead ov windas i| 'as mirras.
My view is our fla|s lookin' back a| me
an'tha sky beyind us an'tha trees in the reck –
you woo|n't know'em na, they've got sa'big –
like summink royal – craaned in sunli|e. Our parst
is awl in fron| ovvus, jus| like tha fewcher,
and of a ni|e, tha moon, nevver still.

MILK MOON

Milk moon, our mother is gone. We have looked everywhere.
All we can see is the she-wolf. Somewhere, I read that it all
depends on how wide we open our eyes. Corn moon, lately we
have only been able to make out the bare outline of something.

Milk moon, you shine your light on the pub. My neighbour
came round this afternoon with some bulbs. We will plant them
any day now. They will grow. Corn moon, our mother is dead.
This is the time for this.

PORTRAITS OF WOMEN – EAST LONDON 1888

Mary Ann (Polly) Nicholls

The locksmith's daughter has a heart shaped face. Her chestnut
hair is pinned back in the style we all wear. Her fringe is two
curls, which fall half way down her forehead. Her eyebrows are
comet-shaped. Her lips are full but not wide and she likes a gin.
Her eyes are grey. She keeps her things neat, and tonight she has
a new black bonnet made of straw and trimmed with velvet.
The docks are on fire; the flames have turned the sky red. We can
see this from the pub. Her nose is small. Her feet are small. She
doesn't mind the shadows thrown from Buck's Row. She'll find
her doss. She'll be back in a minute. Keep the bed warm.

Annie Chapman

Her movements are, eventually, always easterly. Steady, sturdy,
she walks, always circling that idea, with a good wide stride. Her
face is round. Her eyes are blue. Her dark brown hair is curly. It
holds pins tolerably. Her fringe is thick and long. Her lips are full.
She is pale. She is dying and will do what she wants. Crochet, she
loves to crochet – but where is the hook? She does not drink
except for rum. She moves with the ghost of a young girl beside
her. Her son is a cripple. Her daughter has run away to the circus.
The fences along Hanbury Street are five feet tall. She is five feet
tall. *See that Tim keeps the bed for me.* Twenty-nine is her favourite
number. She always sleeps at number twenty-nine.

Elizabeth Stride

Tall, this one, and Swedish. She says her husband and children were killed in a steamboat crash, but that is a lie. Now, she is living with a waterman. Her jacket is fur-trimmed. She has been eight times before the magistrate in twenty months. Her ears are elves ears. Her eyes grey. Her long face ends in a neat bulbish chin. Her mouth is wide and held in a smile and her dark hair flicks in outward curls. She does not understand The Bible. We call her Long Liz. She has her doss. She earned it cleaning. She keeps a key in her petticoat pocket. It is for the padlock the waterman uses to try to make her stay.

Catherine Eddowes

The tinplate worker's daughter has come south, from Wolverhampton. She has had her share of husbands, the gallows balladeer (whose initials she has tattooed on her arm) and the lampblack packer, and now she is with a fruit seller who has a dodgy cough. They sleep at Cooney's lodgings and spend the summers hop picking. She is short and slim with brown eyes and dark red hair. She has been arrested for impersonating a fire engine down Aldgate. We all saw it happen. The fruit seller loves her; they have never had a row despite her famous temper. She is an educated woman. She wears no fringe, her eyebrows are owlish. She has gone to find her daughter who has flown since last time and left no forwarding address.

Mary Jane Kelly

She is Irish, this girl, but speaks fast, in Welsh. Big handed and tall, she has thick blonde hair, with a fringe that flops long on one side. Her eyes are blue. Her man is a porter at Billingsgate, or was. She has been loved by many men and I am telling the truth: really loved. Even by some who paid good money. I am truthful, as she is, always, and that can be hard. Her song is 'A Violet from Mother's Grave'. The flower seller hates it and cannot sleep. She has a way of standing on the street, as if she were on a stage. Miller's Court is her haven and where a girl in trouble can find her. 'The fisherman's widow' adorns her fireplace wall. Her apron is always spotlessly clean.

THE FINDERS OF LONDON

Mud Lark

Many a time I have seen them young women and matrons too
crawling out of the darkness between the barges, and wading
up to their knee and far deeper, in black mud, even when it was
thickly filmed over with ice.

A.J. Munby

There are lines and lines of sound falling in layers.
She's below the line of café chatter,
neighs of laughter, bleeps of tills, phones,

below the line where kids and dogs live
to bark, sing, shout for the ball, the stick;
but it's here that she starts from; her sound

is the creak of rusting iron gate hinges
and the scrape of gate on concrete and silence
as all the layers stop. *What the bleedin' hell . . .*

The patter of feet on iron stairs rises
slightly as she sheds her shoes and steps
out onto the brown of the beach.

I don't hear the difference between the layers
until I feel them. My foot must touch the sand;
feel the cold wet grains resist my weight

before giving me my foot-shape back, sunk,
a little coffin which might come in handy later.
That's when I know where I am, and can begin.

Sometimes she shuffles, sometimes she plods.
Right now the sand is dry and seems as gold
as holiday sand, as sand in stories.

She shifts her weight to her left heel, draws
a circle with the toes of her right foot.
Squats to examine what she has harvested.

Pebbles, just three, one beige, two speckled,
pieces of glass that arrived with the tide, thrown
from the sides of disco-boats, shone by the river,

four three-inch masonry nails pretty with rust,
some old stems of clay tobacco pipes,
I'll use these for toggles for my pebble bag.

These layers of sound lock in history
as linear as man-time until
a jolt, a door, a mud slide throws it open

to the sky, to the river or makes caves
that can't be bricked up, not even now.
And look – just as it would, to her left,

a small brown door appears in the river wall
under the pier, in the darkest place. She pushes,
but only so far, expecting creepy crawlies

to rush, but nothing, or so it would seem, only
that smell, the one you find behind old brown doors.
She puts her ear to the opening, hears the air's

urgent fragmented whispers: Can you do it,
can you bear it, can you bear not to? Can
you do it, can you bear it, can you bear not to?

Tosher

The sewer-hunters were formerly, and indeed are still,
called by the name of 'Toshers', the articles which they pick up
in the course of their wanderings . . . being known among
themselves by the general name of 'tosh', a word more particularly
applied by them to anything made of copper.

Henry Mayhew

A small brown door appears in the river wall
and this time she's through, passing along a tunnel
of strong brick 'til she comes to another door

made of iron, top-hinged and hanging; so to get
past you must push; and a man's voice says, *push*
if you must, push 'ard, but don't let'em see you.

Tired of peace, she pushes the door and is hurled
against wall; momentarily blinded, gagged by a rush
of wind going the opposite way. She sees

the man in the half light she's let in. His hat
is brown and old and that's all she could tell you
'cause, of course, she's scared, who knows what

will happen. He approaches. *Take these; you'll be*
needin'em. Hands her a canvas apron, a darkened
lantern which he straps to her chest, a bag and

a long hoe. He shows her how to cast light,
both ahead and below, to watch for rats
who may travel in gangs, *show'em respect*

but niver fear and take not more'n they allow,
to block her light below grating or by the shore –
You must niver be seen helse you'll 'ave to cut

your lucky and then you couldn't come back,
not niver. He shows her all the uses of the hoe;
how to test the ground, rake mud, save herself.

He says, *listen for water, watch the tides,*
follow your nose – if you find your whack
you'll niver mind 'ow the wind blows for the rest

of your life, then lastly, *rule number one: 'Niver*
travel halone, – 'ceptin', as you 'ave no choice.
He's gone. It's so dark. She flicks open

the shade of her lantern, lighting the tunnel ahead
a few feet, revealing archways of smaller tunnels
branching off the Main to somewhere she

must go. But which? To where? How will she know?
She follows her nose until – a familiar smell,
rosemary or pine, floats by and she follows 'til

the whisper of something like a voice stops her.
Rope and bone, rope and bone, you're not
alone, you're not alone. This she takes

as a sign and turns East below Narrow Wall.
The whisper persists. Her feet are damp and slimy.
Where is the tide? She thinks. *I was promised water.*

Her lantern flickers, she takes out the candle,
places it on the hoe and holds it out into
the distance, when it comes back still alight

she knows that the air at least is safe but still
her breath is laboured, she moves more slowly,
heavy now, eyes wider than the flame,

so it's only now that she sees – though it's been there
for ages – a copper throne threaded with silver,
too solid, too heavy for Toshers to take, rising

out of the brickwork to almost the ceiling and as she
approaches she raises her hands as if in prayer
and then her eyes are met by two small eyes,

rat eyes, and though startled she's neither surprised
nor afraid and the rat says, *Welcome to our little*
lurk, rest awhile, you're in lavender now.

He invites her to sit, then sits beside her, claps
his hands and a thousand rats emerge from
the dark, scurrying, swarming around her throne

and as each passes her feet it leaves something
for her; old coins, nails, ropes, bones,
and each, after giving, licks her dirty feet

and passes to the back of the throng. She thanks
each one very much, admires each gift,
then the King, who is beside her, says,

Good Toshers who don't flam get treated nice
down here. But, don't you be a dollymop;
each ding, each gift is a lesson, take them away,

study hard. Learn them by touch, smell,
whatever; but learn their value. We are family,
you must find your way back. Don't be a stranger!

He crowns her with a rusty tiara and the rats
cheer and everyone sings a song about love
and when it's all over they disappear and then

she hears it – the roar of fast water; crashing
through tunnels but which, where? She runs back
the way she hopes she came, clutching her bag,

gripping the hoe, but the water is faster. She looks
back and sees it – this giant white fist
filling the tunnel, and she's down, and drowning

in too many thoughts when as soon as she knows it
she's swept out of the tunnel, out of the Main, and then
with one push through the hanging gate, where the water

calms down, rocks her awhile before a hiccup
spits her through the old brown door, back
onto the beach, and though the beach is warm

and as gold as a story she doesn't stay, she picks
up her bag, lantern and hoe and looks for her shoes
which she finds, right by the pier where she'd left them.

Pure-Finders

*The pure-finders meet with a ready market for all the dog's dung
they are able to collect, at the numerous tanyards in Bermondsey . . .
the pure-finders are in their habits and mode of proceeding
nearly similar to bone-grubbers. They are also a better
educated class . . . who have been reduced.*

Henry Mayhew

She is sitting on the brown of the beach, watching
the river stir itself, when a sound from above
reaches her ear; a dog barks in the kind

of pitch that means play. She looks behind
to the bankside and there it is, a small lurcher,
running along, then turning, down the steps

to the beach, then spinning circles of joy
down to her, where he licks her ear twice
before splashing off into the low of the tide.

He brings back a stone, drops it at her feet,
sits and waits for her to pick it up.
She cups, weighs, drags the pulp of her finger

across the smooth brown whorls, then looks
out to the distance, deciding where to throw
and the dog says, *You don't have to do this,*

it's not a game. Come with me. She follows
him up the iron stairs, along the embankment
towards Narrow Wall and on, east and further

inland, down Union Street. The stone weighs
light in her pocket. She slides her hand in and out
and each time the stone becomes warmer.

This feels good all the way to Snowsfields
so it's not till then that she asks, *Where are we going?*
The dog just smiles and wags his tail, as if he's lost

the power of speech, as if he'd never had it at all
and that's got her wondering and then he's off
down by the flats, across a small park, past

the 'No Dogs' sign, through a black gate, back onto
a street, by a building that smells of leather and then
a sharp left through another gate and they have arrived.

They are standing in an old yard full of broken
bits. She sits down on an upturned bucket.
To her relief, the dog says, *we'll be needing that!*

She asks, *Where are we? Leather Market,* he says.
Near Morocco Street and Lamb Walk.
This is a tanyard and this leather needs tanning.

He brings out a skin of flayed calf, dragging
it with his teeth, and drops it at her feet.
It smells putrid. She coughs, her eyes water

and she's not sure if it's the scent or pity.
The little dog laughs, *Come now, it's easy.*
You have to make that skin smell sweet – like young

birch bark, like ladies' gloves. We can't just leave
him here to rot as if he deserved it.
The task's not hard. Yours are the hands.

Purify him! She looks at the skin
stained with flesh and asks, *how can I do this?*
The dog replies, *use what I give you,*

I am the source of pure. Take the stone
from your pocket. It's a stink stone, a coprolite,
composed of many layers. I have made

my humble contribution, over wolf-shit
from just before my time. Rub it hard
across the skin while I fill that bucket, together

we'll dress this poor calf, make him sweet as ever
he smelt. They work hard for many hours
and the dog tells her the tale of the beasts. It's well

after dark when he says they're done but she
cannot tell, she cannot see. *Sit!* says the dog,
let the sky light our work. So they sit and wait

for what seems like an hour till the sky clears
of night-cloud and here, between the streets,
away from glare, stars emerge in their usual way,

or maybe not? The longer she looks, the closer
they come and there's so many more than a normal
night. Their edges seem sharper, they dip like bowls

and eventually it seems to her that the compound
lens of a very old eye is looking at them
and she looks at the calf and then the dog

who's resting now, chin on paws, so she lies too,
taking one last look at the shape above
before sleep and the morning erase them for good.

FLOWER MOON

While running, Flower moon, while running, I glimpse you.
I am running from Millbank. At Millbank, I sat at the feet of
an old woman. I scraped a blade across her feet and listened
for the sound of her phone. The pulse in my throat was
rolling. It never rang. I am running, Rose Moon, running
from the Tower, where I saw my future. It is too fast.

Rose moon, Flower moon, I must look at you from the corner
of my eye. I am moving too fast and my sight is blurred. Today
I was running; my feet are scoured. Tomorrow I must shift
boxes. I must move earth. Flower moon, this does not end.

OSHUN'S GRANDDAUGHTER IS LOST IN NORTH LAMBETH

She is laughing on full bellows
knees buckling, tears in her eyes
her sides are splitting. Her laugh
so ripe, little flies escape her mouth.
Her breath tastes of honey. Her laugh
is torn. She must run along now.
The laughing policeman is after her.
Please. Don't get her started.

THE SCAVENGER'S DAUGHTER

I pull you towards me, big man
      and so willed, you fold,
curl to fit – foetaling first

then smaller, tighter, till the small
      of your back is arced
and despite every beer

you've ever enjoyed, I can count
      my years on your backbone.
You lie like this – calves against

thighs, thighs against stomach,
      heavy with breath, warm,
and do not dream what I could do,

if the fancy should take me,
      if I felt compelled to bring
my arms tight around you.

NIGHTSTICK FRACTURE

At the museum, in the medieval
section, the bones lie tagged and boxed.
The Curator is present as always.
He begins. *Skeleton (SK 409)*

*is practically complete. The bones
are solid and well preserved.* Long stripped,
the arms lie separate. I ask,
and yes, I am allowed to touch.

This man was my age
and though tall, had rotten teeth.
His legs show he was a horseman
but I am holding his arms.

They do not crumble.
Each is as light as a drumstick
and although they don't look like they'd be
they're smooth under my fingers.

Actually, these are his lower
arms, laid out for the grave.
The left ulna is in two
but the rest are whole.

Look, says The Curator,
at the mid-shafts and sure enough,
each is marked with a fine
line of healing, a bone scar

and if you trace it
from the broken line of the left,
across both arms, you will have drawn
an arrow-tip as I have done.

Now, it's May Day
and we're somewhere else and there's
this boy . . . *No*, says The Curator, *he too*
is a man, look at that fusion

and the length of those arms,
and, *yes*, I say, *sorry, he looks so slight*
standing there, arms crossed above his head,
as riot police slam into him.

And you, what's happening to you?
Does your body become rigid, as you clutch
your banner poles? Or are you, like me,
a stubborn Cassandra who shrieks

what their helmeted ears can't hear?
Or do you face them dressed only in cotton,
a placard stick against their batons?
And is it Seattle, Paris or London?

The Curator keeps all the measurements
but he cannot tell us how to be – just
that our bare arms shame them,
that our bare arms tell the tale.

THE SEARCH

She is lying on her back, head
propped up on a pillow of wood.
She is naked, William Clift makes
a sketch for his notebook. One eye
on posterity, he faithfully draws
her breasts, the tilt of her chin,
the way her hair curls around
the worn wooden block. We see
that her eyes, nose and lips
are puffy and shadowed. We see
there are rope burns around her neck.

She was seen by James Wright and Caleb Stacey,
carrying a bundle that looked like a baby,
near the ditch, and later by a policeman,
Looking very minutely into the water . . .
I asked her if she had lost anything.

Mr Clift of the Royal College of Surgeons
tells us, *This is the face of a murderer.*
And as we all know, hanging's not
good enough; no one could eat her sins,
no one could be that bulgy eyed.
He has mastered the 'necessary inhumanity'
for the job. This is the theatre
and we are here to watch and learn.
The operating table is wooden with
a channel carved in to allow blood
to drip into a bucket of sawdust below.
A wax woman with only half a face
but a whole perfect tear is on the shelf
above them, beside ivory figures with
hinged bellies that can reveal their innards

to those allowed to touch and, nearby,
a cast, naked of skin and fat,
sits beneath a sign saying 'know thyself'.
It's April and warm. The anatomist must
work quickly, she may putrefy fast.

'Did I tell you I took the child to be buried?
I never came that road; I never came past
his house that day, nor that night.'

She is twenty-four. She is staying
at Fulham workhouse. Surgeon Holmes visits,
he testifies, *The first thing I asked was*
if she had been suckling a child lately;
she said she had not for two months.
He asks to see her breasts, she shows him them.
I pressed on both her breasts and milk spurted
out . . . she said she kept her milk a month
after her child died in hopes that she might
get a situation as wet-nurse;
I then asked when her child died,
she said two months ago, aged two weeks.

Her musculature is of interest, although
not unusual in female convicts.
Hard hams, which fade to string,
muscles that have clenched to the size
of the toys above his head. He peels her
like an orange, fast and furious through
the skin, then cautious, to the pith,
with simple tools, right to the pulp.

Surgeon Holmes says that the child
found in the ditch had been a month
to six weeks old and dead no more
than a day. *His eyes were a good*
deal suffused with blood, as if
they had been very forcibly pressed;
in fact the eye-balls were both destroyed;
I cannot imagine how that could be done
unless by the pressure of the hand
or fingers – there were no other
marks of violence about the child.

'Did I not say it was born in Chick Lane,
Saffron Hill? I never went through the place
at all till the Sunday, and spoke to nobody.'

Hangings take place on Mondays. It's the big
scaffold at the Bailey, covered in black,
the size of a showman's caravan,
it takes most of Sunday to erect and by
evening they start to come, the crowds.
By breakfast the place is humming, all
across Snow Hill and Newgate Market
they wait. What's she having for a last
breakfast? The coffee stalls are doing well,
the pie and pudding sellers arrive. When she
comes out the men will, as they always do,
take their hats off and the crowd will cheer
and sing, '*Oh! My! I think I've got*
to die!' She'd called her son Johnny.

'I had nothing but a gown and two caps
when I went there. I laid in on Saffron Hill
in Chick Lane; my child was a week old
when I got him christened at Spanish Place.'

There is little of her that's round;
well, not in that soft way
that roundness is normally understood,
just her breasts and, since Johnny,
her belly. He slices through one breast,
stale milk shoots – damns his eyes –
then flows down the channel, into
the bucket below. He cuts her again.
Her ribs are stretched and open,
Newgate tulips, droopy from the noose.
He takes her lungs and heart,
weighing each in his hands, exploring
their density and stench. It's getting messy,
a new bucket must be fetched
before he can explore her womb.

'He was a fortnight old when he died;
I got him buried at St Mary-le-bone church;
I was ill for a week after that, and was never
out of doors. I told the gentleman
I had no one to look for the woman
who took the child to be buried; she moved,
and nobody knew where she was gone.
My child was buried in High Street, Mary-le-bone,
in an old burying ground. The woman,
whose house I laid in at, took him
with her son to be buried; her husband

worked in the country. I never went
into that road on the Saturday. I am
as innocent as a baby unborn,
and leave it to the gentlemen of
the Court to look into my case,
for I have not a person in the world
to do anything for me. I told the gentleman
everything the moment he took me.'

Her womb is surprisingly empty.
Nothing there for him at all
just string, pulp and stale blood.
He asks for a third bucket
and plunges his hands into what's left,
searching one last time.

BLUE MOON

When you appear twice in one month, they call you Blue, Blue Moon and then you have no other names. And every sad song that ever was sung, every cheap sad song makes those who hear it remember every cheap sad thing that happened in that sad, sad month, and it's all they can do to leave the pub while they can still see to cross the road.

A mouth has grown in the back of my head, Blue Moon. It speaks to me. It says I must lay, face down, in the back yard, after dark – not worrying what the neighbours think, and wait 'til those hard little eyes form that can look up at you without cloud cover to protect them.

CHIMNEY

Having walked through woods, having left the oak root,
having trudged through snow so crisp it made my feet burn,
I am standing in the hall and looking at the pages of a book.

The word I am here for is 'chimney' and I see a tall
dark chimney rise before me. It is a house chimney.
It is on a dark town house. The house has railings,

three floors and a basement for servants and servants
come and go and I am not one of them and I do not
live here. I do not know where I live. Merely

that if I ask I can find out what this is all about.
The snow-melt slides from my feet and forms a puddle.
There is no bridge or stepping stone, and no trowel.

THE GATE-KEEPER

I think I woke;
at least, I think I'd been asleep,
when the gate-keeper came.

I got busy;
collecting up bones, shaking mud
from my flesh, as was expected.

After, I sat
beneath the lilac, breathing it, chewing
the leaves, refreshing my breath,

holding my bundle
of body and the plumb-bob which dangled
from my hand. He watched.

The gate-keeper
doesn't speak. He never said.
It was someone else's voice

that warned me –
keep the plumb-bob straight. I flinched,
dropped everything.

I began again;
collecting up bones, shaking mud
from my flesh, as was expected.

OBJECTS OF DAILY USE

All day I've thought: what
can I show The Curator
to complement your triple eye?
Each pupil a different shade,

each lid a different droop.
I have a globe of the moon
mapped in Spanish, with a dent
across the flat dark plain.

You have a heart of breccia,
burnt brown and red.
You have hair rings,
circles of hand-cut stone. How

do you wear them? I have three
fish on a stainless steel
pin which I wear just so.
We both have fragments of linen.

LEARNING TO LISTEN ON THE THAMES BEACH
for Mimi

I like to look; you tell me I must also listen.
I scan the beach for iron and try to listen.

Tide holds for just so long then drops its flotsam –
mudlarking's in my blood: I'll try to listen.

The stones, nails, shoes, this one old mitten;
they all could have some meaning if I listen.

Sky that gulls love, the lukewarm sun of Whitsun,
only stand for what they are; unless I listen.

The river arcs its back, its lyric's written,
sings the song of tides to those who listen.

As night draws in and the birds of Hackney quieten
know that Anna sits in Lambeth trying to listen.

LOWER MARSH SPEAKS

Armed with bags and riddles, they head my way;
shoppers, shepherds, mudlarks. It's dark and late.
Shadows stick to me, watchful as ever.
Think I come up with the vinegar boat?

Through sandstone slabs, I feel their footprint, lighter
than of late, less of them, but not as light as at first
and voices, I hear their voices but muffled now.
Has the cat got your tongue?

Around my heart, water, around my flanks,
water; the lambs that drank here, that ate my grasses
lie quiet beneath me and dirty-faced children call,
is she coming back that way?

FROM PAUL'S WHARF STAIRS

Here, where the trail of blue ribbon
runs out, where the pavement is cracked;
here by the river, on the north bank
by the old wooden stairs – slippery
with green, this is the place. This
is where we are. Our eyes, blank, lack
sleep, till we close them and leap back –
flip, fall, enter the world of the river.

We are fluid, gilled, long bodied, flesh
and teeth, till we reach the mud and next,
this being not the end, down we sink
bellies first, our long, long arms, our legs
grown ever longer, reaching, stretching,
taking root. This is how we map our city.

HAY MOON

A man came to visit me, Hay Moon. He was searching for
something I didn't understand. He went again and came back
with a ladder. He went to the top of our flats – below the roof.
The roof, where once I saw a bat and thought it was a bird and
stared long, rooted by its apparent panic. Thunder moon,
when he'd traced his line through all the attics of the street –
he found what he wanted.

Hay Moon, my home is upside down. Only the cat will sleep.
If I stand where the man stood I can see you – solid through
heavy clouds that weigh so much you look stretched. Hay
Moon, Thunder Moon, when will you break through?

AGNUS

Lamb, I have seen you from trains.
I have seen you as I walked through fields.
You looked back at me, raised
your left hoof towards me in a delicate way.
Lamb, I have found your winter curls
by the roadside, on thorns and on barbed wire.

Lamb, who exalts what the world gets wrong,
its failings, its struggles, honourable lamb
feel for us.

Lamb, all winter I wear black to absorb the sun.
Red is not as good at this. It is only for inside.
Lamb, my mother had a dream,
the whole family lived separately in sheds
in the back yard. It was dark and cold.
When we went to find each other, we weren't there.

Lamb, who exalts what the world gets wrong,
heals wounds, smoothes troubles, loving lamb
feel for us.

Lamb, these derelict testaments are stained.
They're cased in walls of clay. We cannot reach them.
We are damp and raucous, our marsh overgrown.
The trees under our pavements are dead. The stairs,
by which you left to sail up river, lead nowhere.
Lamb, why do we fear ourselves?

Lamb, who exalts what the world gets wrong,
crowns hags, creates doubt, fragrant lamb
give us peace.